Who Is Jesus?

A SIX-WEEK STUDY FOR TWEENS

Abingdon Press
Nashville

HOW TO USE THIS BOOK

Who Is Jesus? is a short-term study, consisting of six (6) sessions that may be adapted to various settings. This study looks at Jesus as our Lord and Savior and what that means to Christians and, in particular, to tweens.

Who Is Jesus? gives tweens a good look at Jesus' meaning in our lives before they become youth. It can be used with new Christian tweens to help them understand who Jesus is, thereby making all future contacts with Christianity more understandable.

Who Is Jesus? may be used with tweens in a variety of settings. It is designed to be used with fifth- and sixth-grade students, with optional use with seventh-grade students.

SETTINGS

- Sunday school
- Wednesday nights
- Short-term studies coinciding with other short-term church events
- Study for those new to Christianity
- Pre-confirmation
- As an overview of Jesus before doing the *Choosing to Be a Christian* study

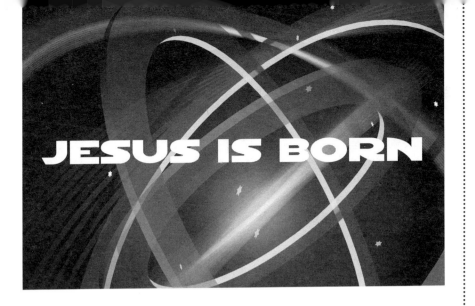

JESUS IS BORN

THE MAIN IDEA

Jesus is God with us.

THE GOALS

Tweens will
• celebrate Jesus as God's greatest gift.
• know that Jesus is God's promised Messiah.
• recognize that God loves us.

THE BIBLE

Isaiah 7:14; 9:6; 11:1; Hosea 11:1; Micah 5:2; Matthew 1:1–2:15; Luke 1:1–2:21

THE PLAN

Get Ready

What do all of these Old Testament prophets have to to do with the Christmas story? Everything! It is the prophets who bring God's word that there is hope for a people estranged from God. This hope comes to us as the Messiah, the Savior, the one sent from God, "God with us." It is Isaiah who tells us that the Messiah will come from the "stump of Jesse." Jesse was David's father. Jesus was a descendant of King David.

PREPARE YOUR SESSION

STUFF TO COLLECT

- **Bibles**
- markers
- nametags (or pins and paper to make nametags)
- scissors
- paper (white or colored copy paper or construction paper)
- various markers, glitter glue, and other decorating media
- masking tape
- paper
- index cards or scrap paper
- pencils
- candle and butane lighter
- **Reproducible 1A,** p. 11
- **Reproducible 1B,** p. 12
- **Reproducible 1C,** p. 54

For Cool ❄ Options

- markerboard
- markers
- small- to medium-size boxes (one per tween)
- scissors
- clear tape
- wrapping paper

STUFF TO DO

1. Copy Reproducible 1A (one set per team), cut the cards apart, and mix up each set.
2. Copy Reproducibles 1B and 1C (one set per team), and cut the cards apart. Mix up each set of "People Cards" (Reproducible 1B).

It is for us to acknowledge our need for a savior and to accept that God loves us enough to send us one, then to celebrate God's love for us shown in the birth of Jesus.

Regular Sunday school attendees will be familiar with the Christmas story, but they might not have made the connection to Jesus' birth having personal meaning for them. New Christians may not have sorted out all parts of the story, and they certainly don't know how to make connections to the prophetic Scriptures. Help the tweens sort out Christmas holiday traditions so that they can discern secular traditions that are just for fun from Christian ones that have to do with preparing our hearts to accept God's love.

GET STARTED

Christmas Traditions Time: 5 minutes

- Give everyone (including leaders) a nametag.

- Ask the tweens to use markers to write their name on the tag, along with the first thing that comes to mind when they hear the word *Christmas*.

- Have everyone introduce himself and tell about one of his family's Christmas traditions.

Ask: Special Christmas memories often involve giving and receiving gifts. If you could give a really super gift to someone, what would it be and to whom would you give it?

- Allow time for answers.

Say: When we gather at church to celebrate Christmas, we are reminded that the birth of Jesus is the greatest gift that we will ever receive. During the weeks leading up to Christmas, we remember the Old Testament prophets who told about God's promise to send a messiah.

DIG IN

Prophecy to Promise Time: 10–15 minutes

Connect Old and New Testament messianic Scriptures and their message.

- Copy and cut apart the "Scripture Match Cards" (**Reproducible 1A**, p. 11), one set for each team.

STUFF—CHRISTMAS TRADITIONS

- ❏ markers

- ❏ nametags (or pins and paper to make nametags)

STUFF—PROPHECY TO PROMISE

- ❏ **Bibles**

- ❏ **Reproducible 1A**

- ❏ scissors

- Divide the tweens into teams, and give each group a set of the cards (mixed up) and Bibles.

- Explain that God sent prophets to Israel centuries before the birth of Jesus, telling of a messiah to come.

- Challenge the teams to match the Old Testament Scripture with the New Testament Scripture and with their common message. See which team can match them the quickest and most accurately. (See answers on p. 64.)

Emmanuel Letters   Time: 10 minutes

Emphasize the meaning of *Emmanuel* while the tweens help you create the worship space.

- Explain that *Immanuel* with an "I" and *Emmanuel* with an "E" mean the same thing: "God is with us."

- Assign each tween one or more letters of the word *Emmanuel*, and give each tween a sheet of paper (white or colored copy or construction paper) for each letter.

- Ask each tween to draw her assigned letter very large on the paper and decorate it with markers, glitter glue, and so forth.

- Place the word on the wall above the worship table.

Bible or Tradition? Stand Up/Sit Down
Time: 2–3 minutes

- Have the tweens sit in a circle.

- Read the events below, one event at a time, that are associated with the Christmas story. Have the tweens stand up if they think that the event is found in the Bible (B) and sit down if the event is not found in the Bible but is an understood part of the Christmas tradition (T). After the tweens have chosen their position, tell them the correct answer.

An angel told Mary that she would have a baby. (B)

An angel in a dream told Joseph that Mary's baby is from the Holy Spirit. (B)

Three wise men visited Jesus. (T)

The shepherds heard about Jesus' birth from the angels. (B)

Jesus was born in a stable. (T)

STUFF—EMMANUEL LETTERS

❑ paper (white or colored copy paper or construction paper)

❑ various markers, glitter glue, and other decorating media

❑ masking tape

STUFF—BIBLE OR TRADITION? STAND UP/SIT DOWN

❑ none

Note: Although several of these events are not explicitly stated in the Bible, it does not mean that the event did not happen as portrayed. Many details are part of the first-century church tradition.

Mary rode a donkey to Bethlehem. (T)

The wise men brought gifts of gold, frankincense, and myrrh. (B)

The innkeeper said, "There is no room in the inn." (T)

Jesus was born in Bethlehem. (B)

The wise men rode on camels. (T)

There were cows and sheep in the stable. (T)

Herod was the king when Jesus was born. (B)

The wise men saw baby Jesus in the manger. (T) (According to Scripture, Jesus was about two years old when the wise men visited him in a house.)

Treasure Hunt Relay Time: 15 minutes

Copy and cut apart the "People Cards" and the "Treasure Hunt Clue Cards" (**Reproducibles 1B and 1C,** pp. 12 and 54), one set for each team. Mix up each set of "People Cards," and place them on a table on one side of the room.

- Divide the tweens into two or more teams, having each team line up single file on the side of the room opposite the table.

- Give Clue 1 to the first player on each team. Have the team find the answer to the clue by looking up the Bible reference and the first player run to find the correct People Card and then return to the line.

- If the correct card is selected, give Clue 2 to the second player and repeat. If the wrong card is selected, the player must return with a correct one. (See answers on p. 64.)

- Continue until one team has completed the story.

Say: In the Book of Matthew, Joseph is reminded of the prophecy that a baby would be born and named Emmanuel, which means "God is with us." From the beginning, God has always been there for the people. The birth of Jesus means that God is truly present, to save the people from their sins.

Near or Far? Time: 10–15 minutes

Tape to a wall a piece of paper with the word *God* on it.

Say: A sin is something we do that hurts our relationship with God. It separates us from God.

✳ COOL OPTION: Hand out a People Card or Clue Card to each tween. If there are fewer tweens than cards, make sure that the distributed cards are matches (for example: Clue 1= Isaiah, Clue 2=Joseph). On "Go," have the tweens try to quickly find the person who has their match. You may have to participate if you have an odd number of students. Repeat with new cards as necessary.

Teacher Tip: All references need to be looked up to find the correct one for some clues.

STUFF—NEAR OR FAR?

❑ paper with the word *God* on it

❑ masking tape

- Ask the tweens to stand as a group at the wall opposite the word *God*.

- Explain that, as you read each situation, each of them is to decide for himself how the situation affects a relationship with God.

- If he believes that it would separate a person from God, he moves away. If he feels that it would bring a person closer, he moves closer to God. If it is something that wouldn't affect the relationship either way, he just stands still.

  1. Spreading rumors

  2. Reading the Bible

  3. Cheating on a test

  4. Running in the hallway

  5. Speaking politely to others

  6. Not doing your homework

  7. Lying about not doing your homework

  8. Helping collect canned goods for a food pantry

  9. Shoplifting

- When finished, sit down and go through each situation, asking why it brings us closer, takes us away, or doesn't affect our relationship with God.

- Remind the tweens that sin caused the Israelites to become separated from God. Because the Israelites sinned, they needed a Savior. Because we sin, we need a Savior also.

What Does It Mean? Time: 10 minutes

- Remind the tweens that God's gift of Jesus means, among other things, that we are never alone. God cares about us, and God sent Jesus to save us from our sins. These promises were not just for the people in Bible times but for each of us today.

Say: Remembering that these promises from God were fulfilled in the birth of Jesus reminds us why Jesus is—and always will be—the best Christmas present ever.

- Have each tween write on an index card or a scrap of paper one word or phrase that tells what it means for

STUFF—WHAT DOES IT MEAN?

❏ index cards or scrap paper

❏ pencils

COOL OPTION: Gather the gift cards or papers. Have the tweens take turns trying to guess each tween's gift by playing a *Wheel of Fortune*-type game. Use a markerboard to draw an underscore for each letter of each word or phrase, leaving a space between words. Players take turns guessing the letters to figure out each tween's gift.

COOL OPTION: Divide the tweens into teams of three or four. Provide small- to medium-size boxes (one per tween), wrapping paper, scissors, and tape. After the tweens have written their gift on a piece of paper, have the tweens place their "gift" in a box and then race to see which team can get their boxes wrapped first.

Note: Have a small group? Have the tweens play as individuals competing to get their box wrapped first. After the race is complete, have the tweens swap boxes and unwrap the gift to discover what gift they have received. Have the tweens keep the gift for the worship time at the end of the session.

STUFF—WORSHIP

- ❏ **Bible**
- ❏ "gifts" from "What Does It Mean?"
- ❏ paper and marker
- ❏ masking tape
- ❏ candle and butane lighter

Teacher Tip: During the next six weeks, the tweens will be creating a prayer wall by adding a new prayer to the wall each week.

STUFF—GOD LOVES US

- ❏ "Emmanuel Letters" supplies (see p. 7)

them personally that God is with us. What kind of gift has Jesus been for them? (*love, peace of mind, hope, faith, caring, and so forth*)

WORSHIP

Time: 2 minutes

Label one wall in the room the "Prayer Wall."

- Ask a volunteer to light a candle, and ask a second volunteer to read aloud Matthew 1:22-23.

Say: Because of the gift of Jesus, we know that God loves us so much that we are never alone; that we always have someone to turn to; that we are loved, accepted, and forgiven.

- Invite the tweens to tape their "gifts" onto the wall near the worship center.

- Close with prayer.

TAKE IT FURTHER

God Loves Us Time: 15 minutes

Ask: How do you feel when you have done something wrong? Do you think there is anything you could do that would make the people who love you stop loving you?

Say: When we do something wrong, there are consequences and we do have to pay the price. But that doesn't mean that they stop loving us.

Ask: Whom do you love? Who loves you? What does it mean to love or to be loved by somebody?

Say: If someone who loves you is angry with you, she might be upset; but she loves you no matter what. And you love her no matter what. This is the kind of love God has for each of us and is why God sent us Jesus. God knows that we need help being faithful. Jesus was God's gift of love sent to bring us back to God.

- Repeat the "Emmanuel Letters" craft, using the words *God Is With Us*.

10

WHO IS JESUS?

Reproducible 1A
SCRIPTURE MATCH CARDS

Isaiah 11:1	Matthew 1:1
Isaiah 7:14	Matthew 1:23
Micah 5:2	Matthew 2:5-6
Hosea 11:1	Matthew 2:14-15

The Messiah will be descended from David.

The Messiah will be born of a virgin.

The Messiah will be called Emmanuel.

The Messiah will come from Bethlehem.

The Messiah will be called out of Egypt.

Isaiah	Emperor Augustus
Joseph	Luke
Mary	Shepherds
John the Baptist	Simeon and Anna
Zechariah	Wise men

God is with us.

ⓖⓖⓖⓖⓖⓖⓖⓖⓖⓖⓖⓖⓖⓖⓖⓖⓖⓖⓖⓖⓖⓖⓖ

JESUS AND HIS DISCIPLES

PREPARE YOUR SESSION

STUFF TO COLLECT

☐ **Bibles**
☐ markerboard or large sheet of paper
☐ marker
☐ ball
☐ scissors
☐ container
☐ pencils
☐ slips of paper
☐ masking tape
☐ **Reproducible 2A,** p. 19
☐ **Reproducible 2B,** p. 20
☐ **Reproducible 2C,** p. 55

For Cool ❄ *Options*

☐ **Reproducible 2D,** p. 56
☐ **palm fronds**
☐ **scissors**

STUFF TO DO

1. Copy Reproducibles 2A and 2B for each tween.
2. Copy Reproducible 2C, and cut the cards apart.
3. Copy Reproducible 2D if you will be doing the Cool Option in the "Take It Further" section.

THE MAIN IDEA

We are called to accept Jesus as Lord and to follow him.

THE GOALS

Tweens will
• know that Jesus calls each of us.
• recognize that accepting Jesus as Lord requires us to base our decisions and actions on him.

THE BIBLE

Matthew 16:13-19; Luke 5:1-11; 9:23; 19:8-10; John 11:21-27; 21:15-19; Acts 2:41; 2 Timothy 1:3-7

THE PLAN

Get Ready

Jesus grew to manhood and began his ministry. Like other great teachers of his day, Jesus had disciples who followed him. One main difference in Jesus' disciples is that, in the ancient world, those who wanted to study under a great teacher came and asked to study with the master. In contrast, Jesus called disciples to follow *him*. It was up to the disciples to respond to the call. The same is true for us today: We are called to follow Jesus. A call requires a response.

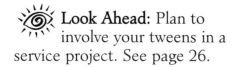 **Look Ahead:** Plan to involve your tweens in a service project. See page 26.

However, as with all disciples, Jesus' twelve disciples took a while to grow into the role. Jesus was so different from what they expected in a savior. At last, Peter declared his belief in Jesus as the Messiah.

Discipleship is important. The teacher can't always be with the disciples. It is left to the followers to carry on the message and the master's work.

After Jesus' crucifixion and resurrection, Peter was charged with the care and nurture of all disciples. Jesus asked Peter, "'Simon son of John, do you love me?' [Peter replied], 'Yes, Lord; you know that I love you.' Jesus said to him, 'Tend my sheep'" (John 21:16).

Disciples are called to do more than learn about Jesus and believe in him. Disciples are to carry the message of God's love and hope to the world. Tweens, too, are called to active discipleship. It's not something you put off until you are "old enough." Tweens are old enough right now.

GET STARTED

STUFF—FILL IT IN

❏ markerboard or large sheet of paper

❏ marker

Fill It In   Time: 3 minutes

Before the session, write the words of today's Bible verse, Luke 9:23, on a markerboard or large sheet of paper. Erase (or leave out) six to seven important words.

- Challenge the tweens to guess what words would fit in each space.

- For each word, give hints such as the number of letters, the beginning letter, or a definition of the word.

- As tweens guess a word, write it in the correct place in the verse.

STUFF—PASS THE BALL CALL

❏ ball

Pass the Ball Call   Time: 5 minutes

Have some fun while introducing the concept of being called by Jesus by name.

- Ask the tweens to sit in a circle, and give one tween a ball.

- The tween with the ball will call out the name of another tween and then tosses the ball to the named tween.

- The tween who receives the ball then calls out another name and tosses the ball to that person.

- Continue until all have had a chance to toss and catch the ball. (The last one to receive the ball tosses it back to the first player.)

- This was your practice round. Begin again, and challenge the tweens to remember the pattern from the first round, attempting to repeat the pattern, but going faster.

- Repeat as there is time, speeding up play each round.

Say: Jesus called his disciples, calling their names because the call was personal. Later, Jesus told the disciples to take the good news to others, calling them to follow Jesus. The call of new disciples never ends.

Accept the Challenge Time: 10–15 minutes

Copy and cut apart "Challenges" (**Reproducible 2C,** p. 55), mix them up, and put them in a container.

- Divide the tweens into two or more teams, and give the teams ten points each to start.

- Explain the following: Every team member must participate in any challenges the team accepts. If a team accepts a challenge and successfully completes it, the team earns a point. If a team accepts a challenge but does not successfully complete it, the team loses a point. If during the game a team hasn't accepted any challenges, the team loses five points.

- If a team loses all of its points, it is eliminated. The team with the most points when time is up wins.

- Have teams take turns drawing a challenge.

Say: Jesus calls us. He challenges us to live as disciples. We choose whether or not to accept the call, the challenge.

DIG IN

Three-Scene Drama Time: 20 minutes

Copy "Three-Scene Drama" (**Reproducibles 2A and 2B,** pp. 19–20) for each tween.

- Hand out the drama, and assign parts to volunteers.

Teacher Tip: You may assign the parts to different tweens for each of the scenes.

❏ **Bibles**

SCORING

After first clue: 10 points
After second clue: 5 points
After third clue: 3 points
After fourth clue: 2 points
After fifth clue: 1 point

If a team guesses incorrectly, it loses 1 point for each incorrect guess.

• Give them time to find and mark their parts.

• Have the tweens act out the drama.

Say: Peter carried out Jesus' instructions. On Pentecost, Peter gave the first Christian sermon.

• Ask a volunteer to read aloud Acts 2:41.

Other Disciples—5 Clues Time: 8 minutes

• Divide the tweens into two teams.

Say: There were many disciples besides the original twelve. In fact, over the centuries, there were so many disciples that we can't even count them. But for now, let's look at just three disciples whose stories are in the New Testament. Let's see whether you can guess who they were.

• Explain that you will give one clue and that each team will confer with its teammates to give a team answer. When the team has its answer ready, the team members are to raise their hand. If not correct, give the next clue.

• See the sidebar for scoring.

Disciple 1: Martha

Clue 1: I gave one of the earliest statements of belief.

Clue 2: I am a woman.

Clue 3: I am very practical and in charge of seeing that the needs of our visitors are met.

Clue 4: Jesus raised my brother from the dead.

Clue 5: My sister's name is Mary.

Disciple 2: Zacchaeus

Clue 1: I sought out Jesus.

Clue 2: I repented of my sins and even paid back four times what I had cheated people out of.

Clue 3: Jesus ate at my house even though many did not approve.

Clue 4: I'm known for being short.

Clue 5: I had to climb a tree to see Jesus.

Disciple 3: Timothy

Clue 1: I was a young man who had never met Jesus.

Clue 2: I was well spoken of by the believers in Lystra and Iconium.

Clue 3: I was raised in the faith by my mother and my grandmother.

Clue 4: I traveled with Paul.

Clue 5: Two books in the New Testament are letters written to me.

- Have volunteers read aloud Luke 19:8-10; John 11:21-27; and 2 Timothy 1:3-7.

Listening, Accepting, Following Time: 10 minutes

- Ask the tweens to think back to when Peter was called by Jesus (in the first scene of the drama).

Ask: **What was Peter doing?** (Fishing, the same thing he did every day.) **How do we hear God's call?** (Other people, the Bible, the church, our own conscience—all help us hear it.)

Ask: Has there ever been something that you felt that you just had to do—something that you felt that you absolutely had to do? If that feeling deep inside is for doing good, for doing the right thing, it just might be God calling you.

Ask: What does it mean to accept Jesus as your Savior? (It means allowing God to influence your decisions.) **Whom do you know who, you think, follows Jesus? What is it about that person that helps him understand Jesus?**

- Together, brainstorm what we do when we follow Jesus, making a list on a markerboard. (We never bully others, we treat others with kindness, we are honest, we try to do what is right, and so forth.)

- Read aloud John 21:15–17.

- Brainstorm as a class about how we feed God's sheep. (Invite people to Sunday school, be there when people need us, visit the sick, and so forth.)

STUFF—LISTENING, ACCEPTING, FOLLOWING

❏ **Bible**

❏ markerboard or large sheet of paper

❏ marker

STUFF—WORSHIP
- ❑ slips of paper
- ❑ pencils
- ❑ masking tape

Time: 4 minutes

- Ask the tweens to sit quietly, and hand out slips of paper and pencils.

- Tell them that they have three choices of what to write for the prayer wall today.

    1. The name of someone they know in whom they see Jesus
    2. Their own name because they want to get closer to Jesus
    3. The name of someone they think needs prayer for any reason

- Ask the tweens to fold their paper in half and to tape it to the prayer wall.

- Close with prayer, asking God to help everyone live in a closer relationship with Christ and God.

TAKE IT FURTHER

STUFF—TAKE UP YOUR CROSS
- ❑ **Bible**

Take Up Your Cross Time: 20 minutes

- Read aloud Luke 9:23.

Say: What does it mean to "take up your cross daily"? It means that every day, in all the ordinary things we do, we keep Jesus first in our hearts, even when it would be easier not to.

✳ COOL OPTION: Follow the directions on **Reproducible 2D,** page 56, to make a palm frond cross to be kept as a reminder of choices that need to be made.

- Give a couple examples of actions that are hard to do but that we know Jesus expects from us, such as choosing not to take drugs, being kind to someone you don't like, resisting the temptation to do something wrong, forgiving someone who has made fun of you, walking away from a bully instead of hitting him.

- Challenge the tweens to give you at least 10 more examples of actions that are hard to do but that we know Jesus expects from us.

Reproducible 2A
THREE-SCENE DRAMA—PART 1

SCENE 1: SIMON PETER'S CALL
(Luke 5:1-11)

Narrator: One day as Jesus was standing by the Lake of Gennesaret, people were crowding around him so they could listen to him teach the word of God. Jesus noticed two boats at the water's edge, left there by the fishermen who had gone out of them to wash their nets. He got into the boat belonging to Simon.

Jesus: Put the boat out a little way from the shore.

Narrator: Simon did as Jesus instructed, and Jesus sat down and taught the people from the boat. Afterward, he turned to Simon.

Jesus: Put out into the deep water and let down the nets for a catch.

Simon: Master, we have worked hard all night but haven't caught anything. But, because you say so, I will let down the nets.

Narrator: Simon and the other fisherman let down the nets and caught so many fish that their nets began to break. They signaled for their partners in the other boat to come help them, and they filled both boats so full that the boats began to sink. When Simon Peter saw this, he fell at Jesus' feet. Simon and his companions were amazed at the catch of fish they had taken.

Simon: Go away from me, Lord. I am a sinful man.

Jesus: Don't be afraid; from now on you will fish for people.

Narrator: With that, Simon, along with his brother, Andrew, and his partners, James and John, left everything and followed Jesus.

SCENE 2: SIMON PETER'S ACCEPTANCE
(Matthew 16:13-19)

Narrator: Jesus was with his disciples in the region of Caesarea Philippi, when he asked his disciples a question.

Jesus: Who do people say that the Son of Man is?

Disciple 1: Some say John the Baptist.

Disciple 2: Some say Elijah.

Disciple 3: Others say you are Jeremiah or one of the prophets.

Jesus: But what about you? Who do you say I am?

Simon: You are the Messiah, the Son of the living God.

Jesus: Blessed are you, Simon son of Jonah, for this was not revealed to you by flesh and blood, but by my Father in heaven. And I tell you that you are Peter, and on this rock I will build my church, and the gates of death will not overcome it. I will give you the keys to the kingdom of heaven; whatever you bind on earth will be bound in heaven and whatever you loose on earth will be loosed in heaven.

Reproducible 2B
THREE-SCENE DRAMA—PART 2

SCENE 3: JESUS' COMMAND TO PETER:
FEED MY SHEEP
(Based on John 21:1-19)

Narrator: After Jesus' death and resurrection, he appeared several times to his disciples. One appearance happened by the Sea of Tiberias, where Peter, Thomas, Nathanael, the sons of Zebedee, and two other disciples were together. They had been fishing all night, but hadn't caught anything. Then, Jesus had them throw their net on the right side of the boat, and they caught a whole bunch of fish. When Peter realized it was Jesus, he quickly swam to shore. After eating breakfast with the disciples, Jesus turned to Peter.

Jesus: Simon son of John, do you love me more than these?

Peter: Yes, Lord; you know that I love you.

Jesus: Feed my lambs.

Narrator: Then, Jesus asked again.

Jesus: Simon son of John, do you love me?

Peter: Yes, Lord; you know that I love you.

Jesus: Take care of my sheep.

Narrator: Then, Jesus asked one more time.

Jesus: Simon son of John, do you love me?

Narrator: Now Peter felt hurt because Jesus asked him a third time.

Peter: Lord, you know all things; you know that I love you.

Jesus: Feed my sheep. Follow me.

WHO IS JESUS?

THE MAIN IDEA

Jesus' teachings are at the heart of who Christians are and how Christians live.

THE GOALS

Tweens will
• look at some core teachings of Jesus.
• practice making decisions based on Jesus' teachings.

THE BIBLE

Matthew 5:1-11; 7:12, 24-27; 22:36-40; 25:35-40

THE PLAN

Get Ready

There is no question or ambiguity in the teachings of Jesus on how we are to relate to God or to one another, especially in the Book of Matthew, where we find teachings such as the Golden Rule and the two greatest commandments. Jesus is clear: Honor God; love your neighbor.

It's more difficult when we get to teachings such as the Beatitudes. These teachings turn our perception of the world upside-down. "The meek will inherit the earth" just seems to fly

☐ **Bibles**
☐ newspapers, magazines, old calendars, printouts of photos from the Internet, and so forth
☐ posterboard
☐ scissors
☐ glue
☐ paper
☐ pencils
☐ masking tape
☐ **Reproducible 3A,** p. 27
☐ **Reproducible 3B,** p. 28
☐ **Reproducible 3C,** p. 57
☐ **Reproducible 3D,** p. 58
☐ **Reproducible 3E,** p. 59

For Cool ❄ *Options*
☐ Scrabble® game

STUFF TO DO

1. Copy Reproducibles 3A and 3B, and cut the letter cards apart.
2. Copy Reproducibles 3C and 3D, and cut the cards apart.
3. Copy Reproducible 3E for each tween.

in the face of American logic. We think that to be meek means to be a doormat, to get walked all over and pushed around. If you look at the Beatitudes (and the Sermon on the Mount) as a whole, you come to understand that *meekness* means putting God and the good of others first. But that doesn't mean being an enabler of bad behavior. The same is true of "the least of these" passages in Matthew 25:31-46. Nations are to be judged by how they treat those with the least—with the least material goods and/or with the least power.

We are to be judged by how we treat those least able to take care of themselves. The way we treat "the least of these" is how we treat God, for the least are also part of God's creation. This is a hard lesson in a culture that has a tendency to blame many of the "least of these" for their own plight. We are taught to "pull ourselves up by our boot straps." Why can't these people do the same? The truth is that life isn't that simple.

However, most of us are generous with our money, giving to many worthy causes. But feeding the least of these is more than about good charity; it is about giving what is really needed. Remember the adage: "*Give* a man a fish, and he'll eat for a day. *Teach* a man to fish, and you'll feed him for a lifetime." Treating people well means going the extra mile.

This session is not about making tweens feel guilty but, rather, to open tweens to the possibility of living a life that is not self-centered but God-centered. Tweens are very self-centered (much like babies, who see the world as an extension of themselves), but they respond readily and happily to chances to give of themselves. Do a service project; it not only helps bring tweens closer to true discipleship but is the best way to build a tween's self-esteem.

GET STARTED

Letters to Words Game Time: 5–7 minutes

Copy and cut apart the "Letters" (**Reproducibles 3A and 3B**, pp. 27–28).

• Place the letter tiles face-down on a table.

• Ask each tween to select four tiles. (An asterisk [*] may be used as any letter the player chooses.)

STUFF—LETTERS TO WORDS GAME

❏ **Reproducibles 3A & 3B**

❏ scissors

✳ COOL OPTION: Bring in a Scrabble® game and play it as suggested in the "Letters to Words Game."

- Play a Scrabble®-like game, having the first player place the first word or phrase on the table and everyone else building off that word or phrase and all successive ones.

- Ask the tweens to think about everything they have learned to do (walk, tie shoes, talk, and so forth) since they were born. Challenge them to work together to create as many words or phrases as they can.

- Whenever they are stumped or have used their letters, each tween may draw another letter to use.

- After a few easy words, have each tween draw a few extra letters. (The number of tweens determines number of letters.)

- Encourage the tweens to rearrange the letters into phrases that tell them things that Jesus taught us, such as *love one another, do good, love God.*

Say: Words are the way we communicate and learn from one another. Jesus left us many words to teach us how to live.

Things I've Learned Time: 5 minutes

- Ask each tween to think of one thing she has been taught (examples: ride a bike, play basketball, ice skate).

- Ask for a volunteer to play a game of Twenty Questions, with the tweens trying to guess what the volunteer was taught by asking questions that may be answered with only a yes or a no.

- Play two or three rounds.

DIG IN

Bible Verse Matches Time: 15–20 minutes

Copy and cut apart all the Bible verse matching cards (**Reproducibles 3C and 3D**, pp. 57–58).

- Shuffle the cards and place them face-down on a table or on the floor.

- Have players take turns turning over three cards at a time.

- If a player finds a match between the first and last part of the Bible verse and the Scripture reference, he is to place them side by side, text-side up.

Teacher Tip: Tweens will understand directions better if they are given one at a time.

STUFF—THINGS I'VE LEARNED
- [ ] none

STUFF—BIBLE VERSE MATCHES
- [ ] **Bibles**
- [ ] **Reproducibles 3C & 3D**
- [ ] scissors

COOL OPTION: With the tweens sitting in a circle, begin handing out both sections of the Bible verses in rhythm. (How many depends upon the number of tweens.) Stay in rhythm as each card is passed around the circle. When the leader says, "Partner," the tweens will scramble to find who has the other half of their verse.

Teacher Tip: To see if a match is correct, have the tweens race to find the Scripture reference to check the answer.

Teacher Tip: The cards and Scriptures are in the correct order (left to right) on the reproducibles.

STUFF—JESUS' TEACHINGS POSTER

❏ newspapers, magazines, old calendars, printouts of photos from the Internet, and so forth

❏ posterboard

❏ scissors

❏ glue

❏ masking tape

STUFF—BLESSED SITUATIONS

❏ **Bibles**

❏ **Reproducible 3E**

Teacher Tip: Most situations can be related to one or more Scriptures. It is not the answers but the connection of our lives to Scripture that is the purpose of this activity.

STUFF—OUR EXAMPLE

❏ **Bibles**

❏ paper

❏ pencils

• If the player does not have a correct match, the cards are to be turned face-down in the same location they started in.

• When all the matches are complete, assign each Scripture to a volunteer to read aloud. Encourage the listening tweens to explain what they think the passages mean.

Say: These are some of the things that Jesus taught us that we need to know in order to live in a good relationship with God and one another.

Jesus' Teachings Poster Time: 15 minutes

Gather newspapers, magazines, old calendars, printouts of appropriate photos from the Internet, and so forth.

• Have the tweens select and cut out words and images that remind them of Jesus' teachings.

• Ask them to glue the cutouts to posterboard to create a montage poster.

• Hang the poster in the hallway where it can be seen.

Blessed Situations Time: 15 minutes

Make a copy of "Blessed Situations" (**Reproducible 3E,** p. 59) for each tween.

• Divide the tweens into groups.

• Assign each group two or three of the situations, and have them decide which Scripture helps them know how to handle each one.

• Bring the tweens back together, and encourage a spokesperson from each group to tell their answers.

Our Example Time: 10 minutes

• Divide the tweens into pairs or small groups.

• Give each pair or group a Bible, and assign one of these four Bible passages to each group: Matthew 5:1-11; Matthew 7:12, 24-27; Matthew 22:36-40; Matthew 25:35-40.

• Ask each tween to think of a modern example of how they can follow the teaching of Jesus. (For those who have teachings with multiple parts, they are to choose only one. For example, one Beatitude or one part of the hungry, thirsty, in prison, and so forth.)

- Have each group report on its example.

WORSHIP

Time: 3 minutes

- Ask the tweens to sit quietly, and give each of them a piece of paper and a pencil.

- Ask them to write the sentence starter "Help me" and to add something they think they need help with that relates to one of Jesus' teaching. (For example: "Help me treat others the way I would like to be treated," or "Help me see the needs of others.")

- Ask the tweens to fold their papers in half and tape them to the prayer wall.

- Close with prayer, asking God to help all to live as Jesus taught us.

TAKE IT FURTHER

"Who Is My Neighbor?" Game   Time: 15 minutes

- Read aloud Matthew 22:34-40.

Say: It's pretty easy to know that God is greater than we are and to think about treating God with respect. But the "love your neighbor as yourself" part is a lot harder.

- Divide the tweens into two teams.

- Have each team come up with an example of a neighbor. Encourage them to be as creative as possible. (The tweens may need examples: the school bully, an old man at church, the kid on the basketball team who always messes up, and so forth.)

- Have the teams play a game of Charades, having the teams take turns trying to guess what kind of neighbor the other team is acting out.

- Have the tweens play as long as time allows.

Ask: Why, do you think, is loving our neighbor as ourself so important? (Because we are all part of God's creation, and it is out of love and respect for God that we are to love our neighbors. It also makes it easier for us to live together peaceably.)

• You may need to explain that *loving* does not mean that you accept bad behavior. Accepting bad behavior is not loving. Those who behave badly need help to become truly reconciled to God.

Service Project   Time: unlimited

• Ask the tweens to brainstorm one service project that they can do together to make a difference.

• Decide on a time frame and who will do what to ensure that the service project is carried out.

❏ paper

❏ pencils

Teacher Tip: You will be the one who has to follow through and make sure that assignments are completed.

Reproducible 3A
LETTERS

A	A	A	A	A	A
B	B	B	C	C	C
D	D	D	F	F	F
E	E	E	E	E	E
G	G	G	H	H	H
I	I	I	I	J	J
K	K	L	L	L	L

M	M	M	N	N	N
O	O	O	O	O	O
P	P	P	Q	X	Z
R	R	R	S	S	S
T	T	T	U	U	U
V	V	V	W	W	W
Y	Y	Z	★	★	★

WHO IS JESUS?

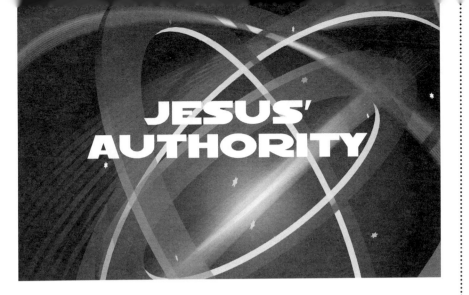

JESUS' AUTHORITY

THE MAIN IDEA

Through the miracles, we are shown that Jesus' power comes from God.

THE GOALS

Tweens will
• be introduced to the concept of the Trinity.
• know that Jesus' authority comes from God.
• acknowledge Jesus' authority over our lives.
• write a statement of belief.

THE BIBLE

Matthew 3:17; John 5:1-27

THE PLAN

Get Ready

The healing of the man at the Beth-zatha (beth-ZAY-thuh) pool is an important miracle story. The story is not so much about healing as it is about Jesus' authority. The waters of the pool were known to heal people of their ailments. The first one in the pool after an angel of the Lord moved the waters would be cured of any disease. A sick man who had been ill for 38 years had been trying to get to the pool when

STUFF TO COLLECT

- [ ] **Bibles**
- [ ] masking tape
- [ ] scissors
- [ ] paper
- [ ] markers
- [ ] round object to trace around
- [ ] pencils
- [ ] markerboard or large sheet of paper
- [ ] clear tape
- [ ] **Reproducible 4A,** p. 35
- [ ] **Reproducible 4B,** p. 36
- [ ] **Reproducible 4C,** p. 60
- [ ] **Reproducible 3C,** p. 57
- [ ] **Reproducible 3D,** p. 58

For Cool ❄ *Options*

- [ ] craft media (See the Cool Option on page 30.)
- [ ] Hula-Hoops®

STUFF TO DO

1. Copy Reproducibles 4A and 4B, and cut the cards apart.
2. Copy Reproducible 4A for each tween.
3. Copy Reproducible 4C for each tween.
4. Have on hand the photocopied and cut-apart cards from Reproducibles 3C and 3D from the previous session. (Make sure that you have them matched up and taped together into complete verses.)

the water was stirred up but had been unable to be first. Jesus commanded the man to pick up his mat and walk. When the man did so, he was cured without even entering the water.

The first problem was, Jesus was healing on the sabbath. Jesus explained, "My Father is still working, and I also am working" (verse 17). The sticking point here for the Jewish religious leaders was that by calling God "Father," Jesus was making himself equal to God.

This brings us to the most difficult theological concept for Western minds: the Trinity. While this story is not itself directly about the Trinity—God the Father, God the Son, God the Holy Spirit—it can help us introduce to tweens what is probably the most important concept in Christianity: God in three persons, equal, without division, yet each functioning differently.

Don't expect tweens to fully understand this concept. Even seasoned theologians don't understand it completely. But it must be introduced and explored if tweens are to come to a true Christian understanding of the nature of God and of Jesus.

GET STARTED

What Does the Symbol Mean? Time: 5 minutes

Copy and cut apart the symbol cards (**Reproducibles 4A and 4B,** pp. 35–36). Tape all eight symbols to the wall, attaching the Trinity symbols near one another and keeping the other symbols separate from them and spaced apart a little bit.

- Ask the tweens to look at the Trinity symbols—without calling them "Trinity symbols"—and to figure out what those symbols have in common. (They are all symbols of the Trinity.)

- Ask the tweens to look at the other symbols, and challenge them to explain what they stand for (the three parts of the Trinity).

- Explanations of the symbols are on the reproducibles. Use them to explain, if necessary.

STUFF—WHAT DOES THE SYMBOL MEAN?

❏ **Reproducibles 4A & 4B**

❏ scissors

❏ masking tape

✳ COOL OPTION: Have the tweens use the pictures of the symbols as examples, and ask each tween to choose a different symbol and make it. Have on hand craft media, such as various kinds and colors of paper, markers, glue, glitter, scissors, chenille sticks (to bend into shape), twine, twist ties, or self-drying clay.

Three-Circle Picture Time: 10–15 minutes

- Give each tween a sheet of paper, a marker, and something round to trace (such as a small plate or a drinking glass).

- Instruct the tweens to draw a picture, starting with three equal-size circles.

- The pictures may be of anything they can imagine as long as it incorporates the three circles.

- Allow volunteers to tell about their pictures.

Say: The Trinity (God in three persons) is at the very heart of Christianity. Today, we will try to understand it a little better. You started your pictures with three equal circles. The Trinity is made up of three equal parts: God the Father, God the Son, and God the Holy Spirit.

DIG IN

Pre-Story Challenge Time: 5 minutes

Introduce the concept of the difficulty of the man at the Beth-zatha pool.

- Designate one spot in the room as the desired place to be.

- Have all the tweens sit on the floor as far from the designated spot as possible.

- Explain that the goal is to get from where they are to the chosen spot while observing these rules:

    You may not use your feet or knees in any way.
    You may not use your hands or elbows in any way.
    You may not be carried or pulled by anyone.
    You may not be helped in any way.

- Expect complaining because the task is impossible.

Ask: How do you think you would feel if you had been waiting to get into that spot for 38 years?

Say: That's exactly the problem the man in today's Bible story had.

- ❑ paper
- ❑ markers
- ❑ round object to trace around

✳ COOL OPTION: Have a Hula-Hoop® relay race. (Hula-Hoops are circles; circles represent the eternal nature of God.) Divide the tweens into at least two teams, with one hoop for each team. Place the hoop at one end of the room or space and have the teams line up single file. Players will take turns doing the following:
1. Run to the hoop.
2. Stand in the hoop.
3. Pull the hoop up and over their head.
4. Bring the hoop back down to the floor or ground. (The hoop may be dropped, but it must be in the original location before moving to Step 5.)
5. Run back to the team and tag the next runner.

❑ none

Teacher Tip: The tweens might think they can roll, but if their feet, knees, hands, or elbows touch the floor, they have to stop.

Beth-zatha Pool Maze Time: 5 minutes

Copy the "Beth-zatha Pool Maze" (**Reproducible 4C,** p. 60) for each tween.

• Hand out copies of the maze, and challenge the tweens to find their way through it. (See answer on p. 64.)

• When the tweens are finished, proceed to "A Question of Authority."

A Question of Authority Time: 10–15 minutes

• Divide John 5:1-18 among volunteers, asking them to read the story aloud as everyone else follows along in their Bibles.

Ask: Why were the Jews so angry with Jesus when he healed this man? (They thought that he was breaking God's Law and that he was making himself equal to God.)

• Explain that they are going to read aloud three Bible verses that angered the Jewish leaders but that help Christians understand the Trinity.

• Ask one volunteer to read aloud John 5:19, one to read John 5:23, and another to read John 5:25.

Ask: Who is the "Son" that Jesus is talking about? (Jesus)

Say: This story explains again that Jesus is the Messiah, the Son of God. If you truly believe, you will let Jesus have power in your life. You will have Jesus to turn to during the tough times.

We Believe Time: 10 minutes

• Quickly review the symbols of the Trinity and the three persons of the Trinity introduced at the beginning of the session.

• Ask the tweens to brainstorm things that they believe about God.

• Record their ideas on a markerboard or large sheet of paper.

• Repeat the process with things they believe about Jesus and then about the Holy Spirit.

I Believe Time: 5–7 minutes

Copy **Reproducible 4A** (p. 35) for each tween.

- Give each tween a photocopy of **Reproducible 4A** and a pencil.

- Ask each tween to choose one of the Trinity symbols and to write something in each of the three places on the symbol. On one space they are to write something they believe about God; on the second space, something they believe about Jesus; and on the third space, something they believe about the Holy Spirit. They may choose from the things that were already listed or use their own thoughts.

- Explain that there is no right or wrong answer. It is personal belief.

- Have the tweens cut out their chosen symbol and bring it to worship.

Prepare for Worship Time: 5 minutes

- Challenge the tweens to state some of the things that Jesus taught.

- If necessary, review some of Jesus' teachings from Session 3.

WORSHIP

Time: 2–3 minutes

- Ask a volunteer to read aloud Matthew 3:17.

- Explain that you will be doing a litany.

- On a markerboard or large sheet of paper, write "I give Jesus power over my life." This is the refrain for the litany.

- Ask for volunteers each to make a statement that begins with the sentence starter "Jesus teaches me . . ." Then everyone will repeat the refrain together.

- Repeat the refrain three or four times, allowing a different tween each time to make the "Jesus teaches me . . ." statement.

- Ask the tweens to tape on the prayer wall the Trinity symbol with their personal statement of faith on it.

STUFF—I BELIEVE

- ☐ **Reproducible 4A**
- ☐ pencils
- ☐ scissors

STUFF—PREPARE FOR WORSHIP

- ☐ none

STUFF—WORSHIP

- ☐ **Bible**
- ☐ markerboard or large sheet of paper
- ☐ marker
- ☐ masking tape

Teacher Tip: Here is an example:

Jesus teaches me that I am to treat others as I want to be treated. **I give Jesus power over my life.** Jesus teaches me to love my neighbor as myself. **I give Jesus power over my life.**

TAKE IT FURTHER

STUFF—IF I BELIEVE

❏ **Reproducibles 3C and 3D**

❏ paper

❏ pencils

❏ clear tape

If I Believe Time: 20 minutes

• Use **Reproducibles 3C and 3D** (pp. 57–58) to begin relating living to belief.

• Lay out the Bible verses face-up on a table. (The tweens will need complete verses, so have all of the parts of a verse taped together.)

• Divide the tweens into pairs or small groups. Ask each pair or small group to choose a teaching of Jesus from among those on the table.

• Explain that each group should try to come up with ways to live in response to their Bible verse.

Example: If I believe in Jesus, and he teaches that I am to treat others as I want to be treated, I would . . .

> . . . never make fun of anyone.
> . . . never bully anyone.
> . . . never steal
> . . . listen to what others have to say.
> . . . do my chores when I've been asked to do them.

Reproducible 4A
SYMBOL CARDS—PART 1

 Entwined Circles—Symbol of the Trinity. All three persons are equal. Circle stands for eternity—no beginning and no end.

 Shamrock—Symbol of the Trinity. All three persons are equal.

 Triquetra—Symbol of the Trinity. All three persons are equal.

 Circle and Triangle—Symbol of the Trinity. Again, the circle represents eternity.

Art: Florence Davis, © 2001 Abingdon Press.

Iris—Symbol of the Trinity. The three lower petals are equal. The third upper petal is implied in art.

Alpha and Omega—First and last. Symbol for God. When used with symbol for Jesus, they become a symbol for Jesus.

Descending Dove—Symbol of the Holy Spirit.

Chi Rho—Symbol for Jesus. First two letters of Greek word for Christ.

Art: Florence Davis (Iris, Descending Dove, Chi Rho), © 2001 Abingdon Press. Randy Wollenmann (Alpha and Omega), © 2009 Cokesbury.

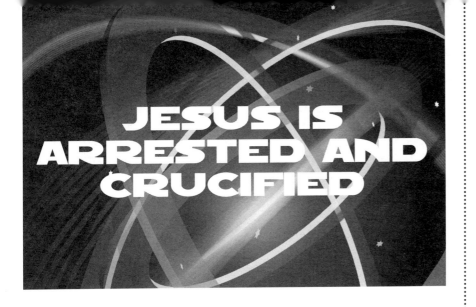

THE MAIN IDEA

Jesus died to save us.

THE GOALS

Tweens will
• talk about sin.
• learn about salvation.
• participate in a meaningful worship experience.

THE BIBLE

Mark 15:34; Luke 19:10; 23:32-46; John 19:23-30

THE PLAN

Get Ready

The story of the arrest, trial, and crucifixion of Jesus are familiar to most Christians, though the order and the details may get jumbled a little. (No one Gospel gives all of the details.) However, new Christians or tweens who attend only sporadically may not know all the details.

The crucifixion of Jesus is central to understanding Christianity. Without the death of Jesus, there would be no resurrection. The Crucifixion is God's ultimate sacrifice for

PREPARE YOUR SESSION

STUFF TO COLLECT

- ☐ **Bibles**
- ☐ scissors
- ☐ markerboard
- ☐ markers
- ☐ black cloth, 7 purple candles with holders, butane lighter, candle snuffer, cross
- ☐ pencils
- ☐ index cards, paper, or sticky notes
- ☐ masking tape
- ☐ **Reproducible 5A,** p. 43
- ☐ **Reproducible 5B,** p. 44
- ☐ **Reproducible 5C,** p. 61

For Cool ❄ *Options*

- ☐ black and brown construction paper, scissors, clear tape
- ☐ purple and yellow construction paper, scissors, clear tape, masking tape

STUFF TO DO

1. Copy and cut apart Reproducible 5A.
2. Copy and cut apart Reproducible 5B.
3. Copy and cut apart Reproducible 5C.

us. It is God's ultimate act of love for us. God allowed Jesus to be crucified and die in order to bring us salvation. From a first-century perspective, it didn't seem nearly as strange as it does to us today. Sacrifice was a part of the worship of God. Jesus' sacrifice put an end to the necessity for sacrifice, but not an end to the need for repentance and forgiveness. We now have a display of God's grace extended to us.

Most of us like to think that we are not sinful enough for Jesus to have died on the cross for our sins. We are more or less honest, we haven't robbed a bank, and we haven't killed anyone. So what have we done wrong?

For most of us, our sins are tied up with where we put our trust—in the almighty dollar, in success, in other people's approval, and so forth. Putting our trust in things of this world and not in God separates us from God, and that is a sin. Many of our sins are also sins of omission: not being hospitable, not treating others as we would want to be treated, and so forth.

However, no matter how small or how big our sins, Jesus' crucifixion is for all of us. All we need to do is truly repent, confess our need for God's grace, and accept God's love and forgiveness.

To understand forgiveness and salvation, tweens must first fully understand what sin is. Doing something illegal is not necessarily a sin. For example, crossing the street against a light isn't a sin, but it's dangerous—and that's why it's illegal. A sin is an act on our part that separates us from God.

The major part of today's session will concentrate on the worship experience, which is combined with the Bible reading. Take time to set up the worship experience so that it can have an impact on your tweens. Let the story of the Crucifixion stand for itself. The final session on the Resurrection can be lighthearted and fun; but to experience the sheer joy of the Resurrection, we must first come to terms with the terrible reality of the crucifixion and death of Jesus, the Messiah, the Son of God.

GET STARTED

Sin/No Sin Time: 10 minutes

Copy and cut apart the cards "Sin/No Sin" (**Reproducible 5A,** p. 43).

• Place the two heading cards face-up on the table, one at each end. Place the other cards in a pile face-down on the table.

Say: A sin is something we do—or even think about doing—that separates us from God. Our relationship with God is hurt when we sin. Let's get more specific.

• Designate one tween to begin.

• First player draws a card and places it face-up under one of the two headings.

• Other tweens will vote whether they agree with the decision. If there are disagreements, encourage discussion.

• Continue until all cards have been placed.

Memorize the Bible Verse Time: 3–5 minutes

• Write on the markerboard the words of Luke 19:10.

• Ask the tweens to read aloud the Bible verse together.

• Erase the last word, and have them repeat the entire verse including the last word.

• Continue erasing one word at a time until the entire verse is being repeated without any written help.

Say: "Son of Man" is the term Jesus used most often when talking about himself. There is no exact definition of "Son of Man," but Jesus used it when he talked about his mission here on earth and when he talked about his own fate. We do know that in this Bible verse, Jesus is referring to himself as the one who came to seek out and to save the lost.

STUFF—SIN/NO SIN
❏ **Reproducible 5A**

❏ scissors

STUFF—MEMORIZE THE BIBLE VERSE

❏ **Bible**

❏ markerboard

❏ marker

STUFF—CLOSER TO GOD

☐ **Reproducibles 5A & 5B**

☐ scissors

Closer to God Time: 20–25 minutes

Copy and cut apart the cards "Closer to God" (**Reproducible 5B**, p. 44). Mix these cards up with the cards "Sin/No Sin" (**Reproducible 5A,** p. 43). You will not need the "Sin/No Sin" heading cards.

• Place the God card at one end of a table and all other cards face-down on the other end of the table.

Say: Remember, a sin is something we do—or even think about doing—that separates us from God. Our relationship with God is hurt when we sin. Let's think about the kinds of things that bring us closer to God.

• Designate one tween to begin.

• First player draws a card and decides whether to place the card close to or far away from the God card. (Does it bring us close to God or separate us from God?) If the card is neutral (such as "eating dessert first"), the card may be placed in a discard pile.

• Each time, ask other tweens whether they agree or disagree with the decision. If there are disagreements, encourage discussion.

• Continue until all cards have been placed.

Say: At some time, everybody sins. We all need help. God sent Jesus to save us from ourselves. Jesus gave of himself to bring us back to God.

STUFF—PREPARE THE WORSHIP AREA

☐ **Bibles**

☐ **Reproducible 5C**

☐ scissors

☐ black cloth, 7 purple candles with holders, butane lighter, candle snuffer, cross

❋ COOL OPTION: If you do not have a cross, have a volunteer cut one out of brown construction paper. Have another tween cut a black cloth (two narrow strips) out of black construction paper. The "black cloth" can then be taped to the cross at the appropriate time.

Prepare the Worship Area Time: 15 minutes

Before the session, gather a black cloth, 7 purple candles with holders, a butane lighter, a candle snuffer, a cross, an open Bible. Copy and cut apart the cards "Seven Last Words of Jesus" (**Reproducible 5C,** p. 61).

• Ask the tweens to set up the worship table, placing the cross on the table and candles in holders in front of the cross. (Give the black cloth to a volunteer to drape around the crossbar of the cross during worship.)

• Ask seven volunteers to read Scripture aloud. Give each volunteer a card that gives the Scripture reference and the order in which it will be read. Each of the volunteers is to look up the Scripture and bookmark it.

- Ask volunteers to be ready to silently remove the candles and the Bible from the worship table. Have a designated place for the volunteers to lay the candles and Bible as they exit the room. Everything should be done in complete silence. (See the worship instructions.)

WORSHIP

Seven Last Words of Jesus Time: 15 minutes

- Invite the tweens to the worship area.

- Ask volunteers to light the seven candles.

- Give each tween a pencil and an index card, piece of paper, or sticky note.

- Ask each tween to write one sin on their card, paper, or sticky note. It can be a generic sin or one specific to them. No one else will know which it is.

- Ask them to tape it to the prayer wall.

- Pray a short prayer asking for forgiveness of sins.

- Explain carefully what will happen next:

  —Seven people will each read Scripture. Once the reading has begun, everything will be done in complete silence except for the reading itself.

  —As each reader finishes reading, that tween will snuff out a candle.

  —When the last candle has been snuffed out, those selected to strip the altar will come and strip the altar of everything except the cross.

  —The last thing to be done will be the draping of the cross with the black cloth.

  —Everyone will leave the room in complete silence.

COOL OPTION: Not allowed to use real candles? Have volunteers cut candles out of purple (the color for Lent) construction paper and flames out of yellow construction paper.

- Tape the cross and candles to a wall.

- Instead of snuffing out a candle, the reader may remove the "flame" from the candle.

STUFF—SEVEN LAST WORDS OF JESUS

- [ ] **Bibles**

- [ ] index cards, paper, or sticky notes

- [ ] pencils

- [ ] masking tape

Teacher Tip: For a memorable worship experience, it is imperative to prepare for it and to give instructions.

Talk About Experiences Time: 15–20 minutes

- Ask those who have participated in some of the Holy Week services that lead up to Easter—Holy Thursday, Good Friday, or Stations (Way) of the Cross—to tell what the experience was like.

- Be prepared to tell the tweens about an experience of your own.

Attend Worship Together

If you are meeting during the Lenten season, make arrangements with your tweens and their parents to attend the Good Friday service as a group.

SIN	NO SIN
cheating	jaywalking
stealing	eating desert first
gossiping	not wearing a seat belt
lying	drinking nothing but soda
committing acts of violence	failing a test

GOD

praying	being kind
reading the Bible	being honest
serving others	visiting the sick
loving neighbors	having an MP3 player
being patient	playing video games

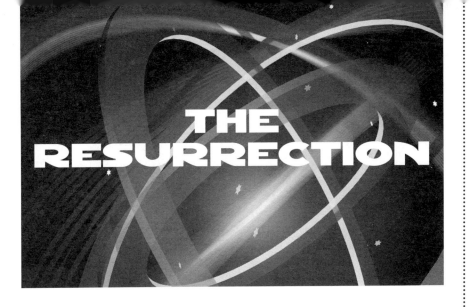

THE RESURRECTION

THE MAIN IDEA

Through Jesus we are offered eternal life.

THE GOALS

Tweens will
• celebrate the Resurrection.
• know that they are offered eternal life.

THE BIBLE

Matthew 28:1-20; Mark 16:1-20; Luke 24:1-53;
John 3:16; 20:1–21:14; Acts 1:6-11; 1 Corinthians 15:5-7;
2 Thessalonians 2:16-17

THE PLAN

Get Ready
The tone of today's session is completely different from the previous sessions. We are no longer mourning the loss of Jesus, the teacher, the friend, the earthly man. Today, we are rejoicing because we are now sure of the Resurrection.

Many tweens have heard and/or read the story of the empty tomb, the two men seeing Jesus on the road to Emmaus, and even the story of Doubting Thomas.

STUFF TO COLLECT

- ❏ **Bibles**
- ❏ cross
- ❏ white cloth and/or flowers
- ❏ white tablecloth
- ❏ white candle
- ❏ scissors
- ❏ markers
- ❏ construction paper
- ❏ bulletin board or markerboard
- ❏ straight pins or masking tape
- ❏ long piece of fabric
- ❏ masking tape
- ❏ craft supplies, such as glitter, glue, ribbon, yarn, buttons, and foam shapes
- ❏ pencils
- ❏ snacks
- ❏ supplies for active games
- ❏ **Reproducible 6A,** p. 51
- ❏ **Reproducible 6B,** p. 52
- ❏ **Reproducible 6C,** p. 62
- ❏ **Reproducible 6D,** p. 63

For Cool ❄ *Options*

- ❏ tissue paper
- ❏ chenille sticks

STUFF TO DO

1. Copy Reproducibles 6A, 6B, and 6C. Cut apart 6B and 6C. Make sure you have one blank butterfly for each tween.
2. Copy Reproducible 6D for each tween.

What tweens may not have put together is that after his resurrection and before his ascent to heaven, Jesus was seen by a lot of people. Yes, his main appearances were to the twelve disciples and to other adherents (like Mary Magdalene). However, did you know he appeared to a crowd of five hundred people?

It is proper to rejoice, to have a party in celebration of the Resurrection and your time together. So, have a good time today.

Nevertheless, it is also important for tweens to understand the significance of the Resurrection for themselves. What is eternal life? It may not mean that we will live in a physical sense in this world forever. When Jesus was resurrected, people didn't recognize him at first just by looking at him. There is something about eternal life that is different. That difference is our spiritual existence with God. Our souls will live with Jesus in the kingdom of God. That's a hard concept for tweens, but let them know that God wants to have a good relationship with them now and forever more. God loves them unconditionally, and that is what the resurrection of Jesus means to us. Jesus is the fulfillment of God's promise of eternal life to each of us.

Today, worship is again very important. It is meant to make the message of Jesus very personal to each tween. Leave plenty of time for it.

❏ **Bible**

❏ cross

❏ white cloth and/or flowers

❏ white tablecloth

❏ white candle

✳ COOL OPTION: Use tissue paper and chenille sticks to make paper flowers to attach to the cross on the worship table.

GET STARTED

Prepare the Worship Table Time: 2–3 minutes

- As the tweens arrive, have them help you prepare the worship table.

- They will need to
  - Remove the black cloth from the cross.
  - Drape a white cloth around the cross and/or adorn the cross with flowers or lay flowers beneath the cross.
  - If you use a tablecloth on your worship table, make sure that the cloth is a white one for today (the color for Easter).
  - Place a white candle on the worship table.

- Optional: Place on the worship table a Bible opened to John 3:16.

Pin the Butterfly on the Cross

Time: 5 minutes

Before the session:

Copy and cut out as many butterflies as necessary (**Reproducible 6C,** p. 62). Write one to three words of John 3:16 on each one. (The number will depend on the number of tweens normally at your sessions.) Make sure the words *everyone who believes in him* (or whatever your version says) are not on cards with other words. Have one blank butterfly for each tween (to be used later).

Cut a cross from construction paper. Attach it to a bulletin board, or draw a cross on a markerboard. (The tweens will use pins or tape to attach the butterflies.)

Obtain a long piece of fabric for a blindfold.

During the session:

• Play "Pin the Butterfly on the Cross" (same rules as "Pin the Tail on the Donkey").

• When all the butterflies are on the cross, have the tweens work to put together the Bible verse, repinning or retaping the butterflies around the cross in the correct order. (They may use Bibles to check answer.)

Ask: Why is the cross now empty? (An empty cross is the sign of Jesus' resurrection.) **Why is a butterfly a symbol of the Resurrection?** (Although the butterfly doesn't actually die, it emerges from the chrysalis to an entirely new life.)

DIG IN

Who? Where? When? Time: 20–25 minutes

Copy the "Post-Resurrection Appearances" chart and cards (**Reproducibles 6A and 6B,** pp. 51–52). Cut apart and mix up the cards. Post the chart on a wall.

Say: Jesus was crucified, died, and was buried. On the third day he rose from the dead. How do we know this? He was seen more than once.

• Lay the cards face-up on a table.

• Have the tweens work together to look up Scripture and discover the answers and to fill in the chart by taping the answers in the correct spots on the chart.

STUFF—PIN THE BUTTERFLY ON THE CROSS

☐ **Bibles**

☐ **Reproducible 6C**

☐ scissors

☐ marker

☐ construction paper

☐ bulletin board or markerboard

☐ straight pins or masking tape

☐ long piece of fabric

STUFF—WHO? WHERE? WHEN?

☐ **Bibles**

☐ **Reproducibles 6A & 6B**

☐ scissors

☐ masking tape

Teacher Tip: The answers are on page 50.

❄ COOL OPTION: Divide the tweens into groups. Give each group a chart and set of cards. Have the tweens race to see which team can correctly complete their chart the fastest.

❑ **Bible**

❑ **Reproducible 6C**
(butterflies used earlier
and blank butterflies)

❑ markers

❑ glitter and other craft
supplies

❑ straight pins or masking
tape

Teacher Tip: If you are *not* going to do the John 3:16 Posters for closing worship, do not attach the butterflies, but have the tweens put them aside for worship.

❑ **Bibles**

❑ **Reproducible 6D**

❑ craft supplies, such as
glitter, glue, ribbon, yarn,
buttons, and foam
shapes

❑ pencils

❑ markers

God Loves Me This Much! Time: 15 minutes

- Use the butterflies from the activity "Pin the Butterfly on the Cross" (**Reproducible 6C,** p. 62). Remove from around the cross the butterflies with the words *everyone who believes in him* (or whatever your Bible version says). This will be replaced with the specific names of your tweens.

- Have the tweens stretch their arms out to their sides as far as they can get them.

- Ask them to repeat together, "God loves me this much!"

- Have them put their arms down, and then read aloud John 3:16.

Say: God loves us all so much that we are offered eternal life. What is eternal life? When Jesus was resurrected, people didn't recognize him at first just by looking at him. There is something about eternal life that is different. That difference is our spiritual existence with God. Our souls will live with Jesus in the kingdom of God. God wants to have a good relationship with you now and forever more. God loves you unconditionally, and that is what the resurrection of Jesus means to us. Jesus is the fulfillment of God's promise of eternal life to each of us.

- Give everyone a blank butterfly, and ask the tweens to write their name on their butterfly.

- Ask them to decorate their butterfly with markers, glitter, and any other available craft supplies.

- Have the tweens place their butterflies above, below, and all around the section of the John 3:16 butterflies that you have removed.

John 3:16 Posters Time: 10 minutes

Copy the poster (**Reproducible 6D,** p. 63) for each tween.

- Put out markers and craft supplies, such as glitter, glue, ribbon, yarn, buttons, and foam shapes.

- Make sure that everyone has a pencil and a marker.

- Ask them to look up John 3:16 and write the Bible verse on the poster, substituting their names for *everyone who believes in him* (or whatever the wording is in the version you are using).

- Encourage them to decorate the poster in a way that makes it personal.

- Hold the posters for worship.

Celebrate Time: 10–20 minutes

- Bring in snacks and/or items to play an active game.

- Celebrate the resurrection of Jesus, the Messiah, and the time you have spent together discovering Jesus by having a time of celebration. Enjoy a snack together. Play a game. Laugh a little. Christians should be filled with the joy of the good news.

WORSHIP

Time: 2 minutes

- Have the tweens hold their own poster or butterfly.

Say: Today, we fill our prayer wall with thanks to God for life eternal.

- Ask the tweens to attach their personal poster or butterfly to the prayer wall.

- Explain that when they leave, they are to take their poster or butterfly with them and post it where it will be a constant reminder of how important they are to God.

- Read aloud 2 Thessalonians 2:16-17 as the closing prayer.

TAKE IT FURTHER

Eternal Life in the New Testament
Time: 10 minutes

- Give everyone a Bible.

- Explain that eternal life is an important subject in the New Testament. It is talked about in the Gospels, but there are many other references also.

- Divide up the following Scripture readings among individuals or pairs to look up and be ready to read to the group:

Romans 6:23
Hebrews 5:8-9
2 Peter 1:10-11
1 John 2:24-25
1 John 5:13
Jude 1:20-21
Revelation 14:6

- Make sure that the tweens read the Scriptures in order.

- After the Revelation reading, explain that the possibility of eternal life is extended to everyone of every age, every race, and every nation. They have but to accept God's grace.

Post-Resurrection Appearances Answer
(Reproducibles 6A and 6B)

SCRIPTURE	WHO?	WHERE?	WHEN?
Matthew 28:1-10	Mary Magdalene and the other Mary	at Jesus's tomb	after the sabbath, as the first day of the week was dawning
Luke 24:13-35 (For when, see Luke 24:1.)	two men, one named Cleopas	on the road to Emmaus (7 miles from Jerusalem)	at dawn on the first day of the week
John 20:19-24	the disciples, except Thomas	in Jerusalem behind locked doors in a house where the disciples were hiding	evening on the first day of the week
John 20:25-29	the disciples, including Thomas	in Jerusalem in a house where the disciples had been hiding	a week after the Resurrection
John 21:1-14	Simon Peter, Thomas called the Twin, Nathanael, the sons of Zebedee, and two other disciples	by the Sea of Tiberias	unsure—sometime after Jesus was seen by Thomas
Matthew 28:16-20 (See also Acts 1:6-11.)	the eleven disciples	in Galilee, on the mountain to which Jesus had directed them	at the time Jesus ascended into heaven
1 Corinthians 15:5-7	first, to Cephas (Peter); next, to the twelve (includes Matthias, replacement for Judas Iscariot); then, to five hundred; then, to James and all the apostles	doesn't say	doesn't say
Matthew 28:11-15	the guard at the tomb	at Jesus' tomb	in the morning (Guards were bribed to say that they had been sleeping.)

SCRIPTURE	WHO?	WHERE?	WHEN?
Matthew 28:1-10			
Luke 24:13-35 (For when, see Luke 24:1.)			
John 20:19-24			
John 20:25-29			
John 21:1-14			
Matthew 28:16-20 (See also Acts 1:6-11.)			
1 Corinthians 15:5-7			
Matthew 28:11-15			

Reproducible 6B
POST-RESURRECTION APPEARANCES

Mary Magdalene and the other Mary	at Jesus's tomb	after the sabbath, as the first day of the week was dawning
two men, one named Cleopas	on the road to Emmaus (7 miles from Jerusalem)	at dawn on the first day of the week
the disciples, except Thomas	in Jerusalem behind locked doors in a house where the disciples were hiding	evening on the first day of the week
the disciples, including Thomas	in Jerusalem in a house where the disciples had been hiding	a week after the Resurrection
Simon Peter, Thomas called the Twin, Nathanael, the sons of Zebedee, and two other disciples	by the Sea of Tiberias	unsure— sometime after Jesus was seen by Thomas
the eleven disciples	in Galilee, on the mountain to which Jesus had directed them	at the time Jesus ascended into heaven
first, to Cephas (Peter); next, to the twelve (includes Matthias, replacement for Judas Iscariot); then, to five hundred; then, to James and all the apostles	doesn't say	doesn't say
the guard at the tomb	at Jesus' tomb	in the morning (Guards were bribed to say that they had been sleeping.)

WHO IS JESUS?

ADDITIONAL REPRODUCIBLES

Reproducible 1C
TREASURE HUNT CLUE CARDS

CLUE 1 I am a prophet who foretold the birth of a messiah. You can find what I said in chapter 9, verse 6. Which prophet am I? JEREMIAH, ISAIAH, MICAH	**CLUE 7** In chapter 2, verse 7, I wrote about where Jesus was placed after he was born. Which Gospel writer am I? MATTHEW, MARK, LUKE
CLUE 2 I was told to name the Messiah Jesus, because he would save the people from their sins. Who am I? (Matthew 1:20-21) MARY, JOSEPH, ZECHARIAH	**CLUE 8** An angel told us where to find the baby Jesus. Who are we? (Luke 2:8-14) ELIZABETH and ZECHARIAH, WISE MEN, SHEPHERDS
CLUE 3 I said, "My spirit rejoices in God my Savior." Who am I? (Luke 1:46-47) MARY, JOSEPH, ZECHARIAH	**CLUE 9** We waited a long time for the birth of the Messiah, and we were in the Temple when the baby Jesus was presented. Who are we? (Luke 2:22-23, 25, 36) ZECHARIAH and ELIZABETH, SIMEON and ANNA, MARY and JOSEPH
CLUE 4 I am Jesus' cousin. I am the prophet called to prepare the way for Jesus. Who am I? (Luke 1:60,76) ZECHARIAH, JOHN THE BAPTIST, ISAIAH	**CLUE 10** A star led us to the young child. Who are we? (Matthew 2:1-2) ELIZABETH and ZECHARIAH, WISE MEN, SHEPHERDS
CLUE 5 I am a prophet who said that my son would be the one who would come to prepare the way for the Messiah. Who am I? (Luke 1:67,76) DAVID, JOSEPH, ZECHARIAH	**CLUE 11** Jesus was named Emmanuel, which means "_____." (Luke 1:23; John 1:23; Matthew 1:23)
CLUE 6 Jesus was born in Bethlehem because a decree went out that all people had to return to the town of their ancestors to be registered. I was the person who issued that decree. (Luke 2:1-4) QUIRINIUS, KING HEROD, EMPEROR AUGUSTUS	

Reproducible 2C
CHALLENGES

Touch your nose with your tongue.	Name the four Gospels.
Walk across the room while balancing a book on your head.	Walk from one end of the room to the other with no help and eyes closed.
Hop on one foot backward across the room and back again.	Name the first ten books of the New Testament in order (without looking at a Bible).
Say the names of five of Jesus' disciples.	Say the alphabet backward.
Sit on the floor with your back against the wall, then stand up without using your hands.	Name the seven dwarfs in the movie *Snow White*.
Do 10 jumping jacks while singing "Twinkle, Twinkle, Little Star."	With your arms straight out in front of you and keeping your feet flat on the floor and your back straight, squat down and come back up without help and without losing your balance.
Sing "Mary Had a Little Lamb" as fast as you can.	Do ten pushups.

Reproducible 2D
MAKE A PALM FROND CROSS

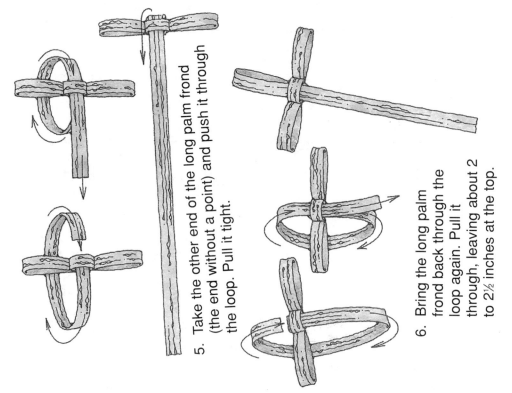

5. Take the other end of the long palm frond (the end without a point) and push it through the loop. Pull it tight.

6. Bring the long palm frond back through the loop again. Pull it through, leaving about 2 to 2½ inches at the top.

You will need:
- one short palm frond (about 11 inches long)
- one long palm frond (about 14 inches long)

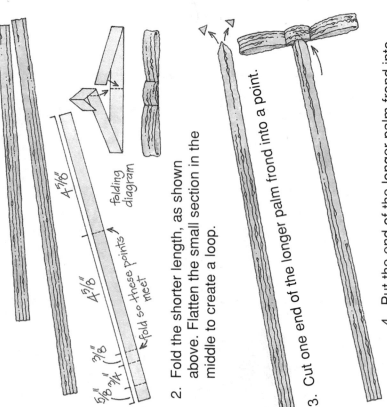

1. Select two palm fronds from a palm branch.

folding diagram

4⅝"

4⅝"

⅝" ¾" ⅜"

fold so these points meet

2. Fold the shorter length, as shown above. Flatten the small section in the middle to create a loop.

3. Cut one end of the longer palm frond into a point.

4. Put the end of the longer palm frond into the loop on the shorter palm frond. (Do not pull it through the loop.)

Art: Brenda Gilliam, © 2001 Cokesbury.

WHO IS JESUS?

Reproducible 3C
BIBLE VERSE MATCHES

In everything do to others	as you would have them do to you.
You shall love the Lord your God	with all your heart, and with all your soul, and with all your mind.
You shall love your neighbor	as yourself.
Blessed are the poor in spirit,	for theirs is the kingdom of heaven.
Blessed are the merciful,	for they will receive mercy.
Blessed are the peacemakers,	for they will be called children of God.
Truly I tell you, just as you did it to one of the least of these who are members of my family,	you did it to me.

Reproducible 3D
SCRIPTURE REFERENCES
FOR BIBLE VERSE MATCHES

Matthew 7:12a	Matthew 22:37
Matthew 22:39	Matthew 5:3
Matthew 5:7	Matthew 5:9
Matthew 25:40	

WHO IS JESUS?

Reproducible 3E
BLESSED SITUATIONS

SITUATIONS	SCRIPTURES
A classmate often comes to school without money or food for lunch.	Blessed are those who mourn, for they will be comforted. (Matthew 5:4)
You are very proud of yourself for winning the spelling bee, and you make sure everybody knows that you beat last year's winner.	Blessed are the meek, for they will inherit the earth. (Matthew 5:5)
	Blessed are the merciful, for they will receive mercy. (Matthew 5:7)
A family member suddenly dies.	
You are being bullied and want to strike back. You want to do the right thing, but you sure want to get revenge.	Blessed are those who are persecuted for righteousness' sake, for theirs is the kingdom of heaven. (Matthew 5:10)
Your teacher asks you to help someone whom you really don't like.	In everything do to others as you would have them do to you. (Matthew 7:12a)
Other kids make fun of you for singing in your church choir.	You shall love your neighbor as yourself. (Matthew 22:39)
You have an opportunity to help collect clothing for a homeless shelter.	Just as you did it to one of the least of these who are members of my family, you did it to me. (Matthew 25:40)

Reproducible 4C
BETH-ZATHA POOL MAZE

There are entrances at each of the five porches or porticoes that surround the pool of Beth-zatha (beth-ZAY-thuh), but only one of these entrances will allow Jesus to visit all five porches without retracing his steps on his way to the pool. Find the correct path and get him into the water.

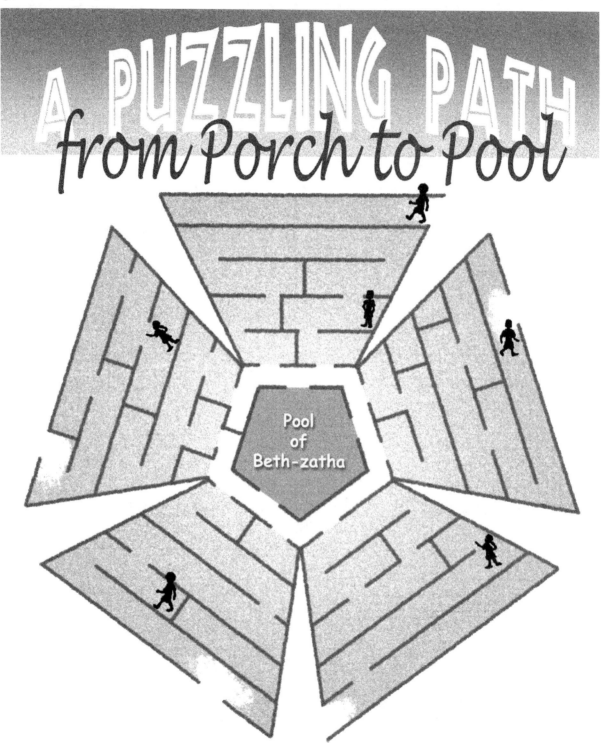

Art: Randy Wollenmann, © 2003 Cokesbury.

WHO IS JESUS?

Reproducible 5C
SEVEN LAST WORDS OF JESUS

FIRST READER Look up and be prepared to read aloud Luke 23:32-38. When you are finished reading, snuff out the first candle.	**FIFTH READER** Look up and be prepared to read aloud John 19:28-29. When you are finished reading, snuff out the fifth candle.
SECOND READER Look up and be prepared to read aloud Luke 23:39-43. When you are finished reading, snuff out the second candle.	**SIXTH READER** Look up and be prepared to read aloud John 19:30. When you are finished reading, snuff out the sixth candle.
THIRD READER Look up and be prepared to read aloud John 19:23-27. When you are finished reading, snuff out the third candle.	**SEVENTH READER** Look up and be prepared to read aloud Luke 23:44-46. When you are finished reading, snuff out the final candle.
FOURTH READER Look up and be prepared to read aloud Mark 15:34. (*It's okay to omit the foreign words, if you don't want to try reading them.*) When you are finished reading, snuff out the fourth candle.	

Reproducible 6C
BUTTERFLIES

Art: Randy Wollenmann, © 2004 Cokesbury.

WHO IS JESUS?

God So Loved the World

Answers

Scripture Match Cards
(Reproducible 1A)

The Messiah will be descended from David.

Isaiah 11:1; Matthew 1:1

The Messiah will be born of a virgin.

The Messiah will be called Emmanuel.

Isaiah 7:14; Matthew 1:23

The Messiah will come from Bethlehem.

Micah 5:2; Matthew 2:5-6

The Messiah will be called out of Egypt.

Hosea 11:1; Matthew 2:14-15

Beth-zatha Pool Maze
(Reproducible 4C)

Treasure Hunt Clues
(Reproducibles 1B and 1C)

Clue 1: Isaiah

Clue 2: Joseph (Mary is told the same thing, but that is in Luke.)

Clue 3: Mary

Clue 4: John the Baptist

Clue 5: Zechariah

Clue 6: Emperor Augustus

Clue 7: Luke

Clue 8: shepherds

Clue 9: Simeon and Anna

Clue 10: wise men

Clue 11: God is with us.

WHO IS JESUS?